W9-AMN-317

J.K.
ROWLING

Author

Joanne Mattern

Ferguson
An imprint of ☑ Facts On File

J.K. Rowling: Author

Ferguson
An imprint of Facts On File, Inc.
132 West 31st Street
New York NY 10001

Library of Congress Cataloging-in-Publication Data
Mattern, Joanne, 1963–
    J.K. Rowling, author / Joanne Mattern.
      p. cm
    Includes bibliographical references and index.
    ISBN 0-8160-5884-9 (hc : alk. paper)
  1. Authors, English—20th century—Biography. 2. Potter, Harry (Fictitious character)
3. Children's stories—Authorship. 4. Authorship. I. Title.
    PR6068.093Z764 2005
    823'.914—dc22   2004013292

Ferguson books are available at special discounts when purchased in bulk quantities for businesses, associations, institutions, or sales promotions. Please call our Special Sales Department in New York at (212) 967-8800 or (800) 322-8755.

You can find Ferguson on the World Wide Web at http://www.fergpubco.com

Text design by David Strelecky

Pages 93–111 adapted from Ferguson's *Encyclopedia of Careers and Vocational Guidance*, Twelfth Edition

Printed in the United States of America

MP Hermitage 10 9 8 7 6 5 4 3 2 1

This book is printed on acid-free paper.

CONTENTS

1

A WIZARD WITH WORDS

Her books have captivated children and adults all over the world. She is one of the most popular authors ever and has won dozens of awards. Whenever she releases a new book, eager readers line up in bookstores to purchase their copies—sometimes camping out overnight to be among the first buyers. Her stories have made her one of the richest women in the world. She is Joanne Kathleen Rowling, author of the phenomenally successful *Harry Potter* series of children's books.

J.K. Rowling published the first *Harry Potter* book in Great Britain in 1997. It was called *Harry Potter and the Philosopher's Stone*. One year later, the book—retitled *Harry Potter and the Sorcerer's Stone*—was published in the United States. The book introduced readers to young Harry Potter, an 11-year-old orphan with a strange lightning-bolt-shaped scar on his forehead. Harry doesn't

Joanne Kathleen (J.K.) Rowling's books have captivated children and adults all over the world. (Landov)

know it, but he is a powerful wizard. He learns the truth about his past and studies how to use magic at a wizards' school called Hogwarts. In the books that followed, Harry learns more about his powers and his mysterious past and prepares to face the dangerous wizard who murdered Harry's parents.

J.K. Rowling did not expect her books to become such a huge success. She did not set out to write a best-selling children's book. Instead, she wrote a story that appealed to her. The fact that it also touched the imaginations of millions of readers around the world came as a complete surprise to her.

The *Harry Potter* books turned Rowling's life into a dream come true. But until the books were published, Rowling's life was very ordinary. She had a happy childhood, attended school, and later became a single mother struggling to support herself and her young daughter. Inside her mind, however, there was nothing ordinary about J.K. Rowling. Like that of many authors, her imagination held the key to a whole new world.

AN IMAGINATIVE CHILD

Joanne Kathleen Rowling was born on July 31, 1965. Her parents, Peter and Anne, had met on a train the year before. At that time, Peter and Anne were both in England's Royal Navy. They met at King's Cross Station in London and fell in love at first sight. They married early in 1965. Joanne was their first child.

Small-Town Life

The Rowlings' first home was in Yate, a small town about 10 miles northeast of Bristol, an important city in southeast England, across the Bristol Channel from Wales. Another nearby town has the interesting name Chipping Sodbury. As an adult, Joanne, who has a writer's natural fondness for unusual names, said she was born in

Chipping Sodbury. However, her birth certificate says she was born in Yate.

Peter and Anne had left the Royal Navy shortly before they married. Peter worked as a production engineer at an aircraft factory in Bristol. Anne stayed home to be a full-time mother to her daughters.

The Rowlings bought a small one-story house on a street called Sundridge Park. During the 1960s, the area around Sundridge Park was full of fields and open space. A park called Kingsgate Park was within walking distance.

When Joanne was almost two years old, she became a big sister. Anne gave birth to Dianne in June 1967. Although Joanne had been born in a hospital, Dianne was born at home. Joanne later said that Dianne's birth is her earliest childhood memory.

Soon after Dianne was born, the family moved to a town called Winterbourne, about four miles away. Winterbourne was more rural than Yate, and the Rowlings felt it was a nicer area in which to raise their children.

Books and Games

Peter continued to work at the aircraft factory while Anne remained at home. She was a devoted mother to Jo and Di, as the Rowling girls were called. One of the family's favorite pastimes was reading. Neighbors would later comment that the Rowling home had more books than any other home in the neighborhood.

Peter also enjoyed reading to his children. Later, Joanne would recall a favorite childhood memory. When she was quite young, she became sick with the measles. To pass the time, her father read to her from *The Wind in the Willows*, a classic British children's book. Joanne especially enjoyed the way the book's animal characters behaved in human ways. This would be an important influence on her own writing: Many of the animals in her *Harry Potter* books have human characteristics.

Jo and Di were especially close. The girls had many friends on Nicholls Lane, where they lived. Two of their best friends were Vikki and Ian Potter, who lived just a few houses down the street. (Later, Joanne would use the Potters' last name in her books.) Jo was the oldest of the four children and frequently was the leader in their childhood games.

The four children especially enjoyed using their imaginations. One of their favorite games was playing witches and wizards. The children borrowed brooms from their garages and ran around the neighborhood, pretending to fly. They used dress-up clothes to look like the characters they played. It was not unusual for the children to end up sitting together while Jo told them spooky stories.

The First Stories

Joanne decided to be a writer when she was very young, but she kept her plan a secret for years. (Associated Press)

Even when she was very young, storytelling was one of Joanne's favorite activities. One day, Joanne made up a story to entertain her younger sister. The story was about a little girl named Di who fell down a rabbit hole. She was rescued by a family of rabbits who fed her strawberries. Dianne loved the story and asked Joanne to tell it over and over again.

However, Dianne was annoyed that Joanne changed or added details every time she told the story. To solve this problem, Joanne began to write her stories down.

Rabbits often appeared in Joanne's stories. She remembers the first story she ever wrote down, when she was five or six years old. The hero was a rabbit named, of all things, Rabbit. He got the measles and was visited by his friends. Like many authors, Joanne took events that happened in real life—such as her own bout with the measles—and transformed them into stories.

Joanne discovered that she loved writing stories. She decided that one day she would write stories for a living. However, Joanne told no one about her ambitions. Her plans would remain a secret for many years.

Another Move

The Rowling family was happy in Winterbourne. However, Peter and Anne had always dreamed of buying an old house and fixing it up. When Joanne was about nine years old, her parents sold the house on Nicholls Lane and moved to Church Cottage in the village of Tutshill, located on the other side of the River Severn, in a wooded area called the Forest of Dean. Their home was a stone house that had been built in 1848 and had once been the village school. Although their parents were happy to be living in an old house in a rural village, Joanne and Dianne were not as excited. Like children anywhere, they dreaded moving to a new home, making new friends, and fitting in at a new school.

Joanne started classes at Tutshill Church of England Primary School when she was nine years old. Her first day at the new school did not go well. Her new teacher, Sylvia Morgan, gave Joanne a math test to see how much she knew. Unfortunately, the test included fractions, which Joanne had not studied in her old school. She scored only half a point on the test. Joanne's poor score led Mrs. Morgan to believe that Joanne was not very smart. Mrs. Morgan had an interesting seating plan in her classroom. She placed the smartest students on her left and the slower students on her right. Joanne was told to sit at a desk at the far right side of the room. "I was as far right as you could get without sitting in the playground," she later said.

Joanne knew she was smart. Now she had to prove it to Mrs. Morgan and the other students in the class. To achieve this, Joanne worked hard. By the end of the year, she had moved into the second seat on the left. Unfortunately, Joanne's improvement at school cost her some friendships, as the girls in her class thought she was just showing off.

Along with school, Joanne took part in many other activities. She and Di enjoyed long walks along the River Wye and through the Forest of Dean. The area was a perfect setting for Joanne's imaginative stories of heroes and magic. Joanne also participated in local organizations. For several years, she was a Brownie and took part in community service projects with that organization.

Lost in Books

Joanne did well in school, especially when it came to reading. Becoming lost in stories was still her favorite pastime. She especially enjoyed stories that featured girls having adventures. Her favorite book when she was a child was *The Little White Horse* by Elizabeth Goudge. Joanne liked the book so much because the heroine was very unusual: She was not beautiful, and she often got into trouble. Perhaps Joanne felt this heroine was a lot like herself.

Another of Joanne's favorite authors was Jane Austen. Austen was a British writer who lived during the 19th century. Her books feature detailed observations of human behavior and society. Joanne also enjoyed books with magical elements. C. S. Lewis, E. Nesbit, and Paul Gallico were among her favorite authors. Joanne continued to love animals and has often said that Anna Sewell's *Black Beauty,* a story about a horse, is one of her favorite books.

Joanne continued to write stories as well as read them. Many features of the books she loved found their way into her writing. She filled her stories with magical characters who had unusual adventures. Despite her enthusiasm for writing, no one knew about her stories except her sister, Di. Even though Di always encouraged Joanne to write, for some reason Joanne was embarrassed about her plan to become an author. Even though writing full time had been her greatest ambition since she was six years old, she felt it was not a practical plan and that people—including her parents—might laugh at her if they found out about it.

Insecurities

In 1976, Joanne graduated from Tutshill Primary School and started classes at Wyedean Preparatory School, a comprehensive school. In England, a comprehensive school corresponds to an American junior high and high school.

At first, Joanne did not feel comfortable at the school. She was only 11 years old and felt lost in the large school, which included students up to 17 years old. Joanne also felt she was unattractive, with a plain face, ugly glasses, and uninteresting hair. She was shy and insecure.

In spite of her shyness, Joanne continued to do well academically. She was always ready to participate in class and frequently raised her hand. Unfortunately, once again Joanne's eagerness to do well academically caused some students to think she was a snob or a show-off. In reality, she was just shy and taking comfort in the one thing she felt she was good at.

Gradually, Joanne began to fit in. Her popularity increased after she got into a fight with a bigger girl at school. Although Joanne claimed that she was leaning against a row of lockers, and that's what held her up during the fight, her classmates admired her for not backing down from the other girl's attack. Joanne discovered that her courage had made her quite famous around school—at least for a few days.

Although she was not part of the popular crowd, she did find a close circle of friends. These friends were a lot like her—shy, serious, and interested in books. As she had when she was a child living in Winterbourne, Joanne became the center of the group, telling stories of her friends and their daring, make-believe adventures. Despite her obvious talents, however, Joanne's longing to be a full-time author remained a secret dream.

3

LACK OF DIRECTION

As Joanne moved up in the ranks of Wyedean Preparatory School, she became more self-confident. As usual, her favorite class was English. Joanne's teachers noticed and encouraged her talent by helping her sharpen her writing skills.

Strict but Fair

Joanne's favorite instructor at Wyedean was an English teacher named Lucy Shepherd. Miss Shepherd was only in her 20s, not much older than her students. Despite her youth, she was strict and very much in control of her class. She expected her students to give her their full attention and once scolded Joanne for doodling in the middle of class. Along with teaching good writing skills, Miss Shepherd was a role model for Joanne as she showed that women could be strong, self-confident, and in charge of their lives.

Miss Shepherd and other English teachers at school were quick to recognize Joanne's writing talent. In spite of this, Joanne still told no one that she dreamed of becoming an author one day.

Another Favorite Author

As she grew older, Joanne continued to enjoy Jane Austen and other classic British novelists. When she

English and writing classes were always Joanne's favorites. Here she speaks to two young winners of a Harry Potter essay contest sponsored by Scholastic. (Associated Press)

was 14 years old, her great aunt gave her a book by British author Jessica Mitford, who was born in 1917 into a well-known, wealthy family but found many aspects of her life to be boring and too conventional. Instead of following the traditional path, Mitford rebelled by running away from home. Soon afterward, she wanted to have a camera to photograph her adventures, so she charged one on her father's credit account without his permission. Joanne loved this story and admired Mitford for her nerve, although she admitted that she would never have been brave enough to do such a thing herself.

A Teenager in Tutshill

Like many teenagers who live in small towns, Joanne found little to occupy her time as she grew older. Tutshill was so small and out of the way that it did not even have a movie theater. While many teens hung out on the streets and smoked cigarettes, Joanne spent much of her time in her room, writing. She also enjoyed drawing and playing the guitar.

Occasionally, Joanne and her family or friends left Tutshill to see a movie or attend a play. Along with her class, she traveled to Stratford-on-Avon, home of William Shakespeare, to see several Shakespeare plays.

Tragic News

Joanne's normal adolescence was shattered when her mother became ill. For some time, Anne had been feeling weak. She had trouble lifting even small objects and began falling. When Joanne was 15 years old, her mother was diagnosed with multiple sclerosis (MS). MS is a progressive disease that can rob its victims of the ability to walk, move, and see.

The Rowlings were devastated by Anne's illness. Although Peter dedicated himself to caring for his wife, and Joanne and Dianne helped as best they could, the girls missed the active mother who was involved in their lives. Joanne took to spending more time away from home in order to escape the sadness there. She also began smoking, wearing leather jackets and heavy makeup, listening to punk music, and trying to act tougher than she felt inside.

Senior Year

As Joanne entered her final year at Wyedean, her life began to settle down. She had befriended a new boy in school named Sean Harris. She and Sean became close friends and constant companions. It also helped that Sean had his driver's license and his own car, a Ford Anglia. The two spent many hours driving around and talking about their hopes and dreams for the future. Later, Joanne would model the character of Ron Weasley, one of Harry Potter's best friends, on Sean; she would even include his car (with added magical powers) in her second novel, *Harry Potter and the Chamber of Secrets*. That book is also dedicated to Sean.

Sean's friendship and a general sense of maturity helped Joanne fit in better at school. During her senior year, she was named head girl. This is a traditional honor given to senior students at British schools, voted on by the students and the faculty. Although the head girl and boy do not have many responsibilities, it is a tremendous honor to be voted into one of these positions. Obviously, Joanne had won the respect and admiration of her fellow students, even though she had felt shy and unpopular during her early days at Wyedean.

Disappointment

As she neared the end of her days at Wyedean Preparatory School, Joanne's teachers encouraged her to apply to Oxford University, one of the oldest and best schools in England. Joanne was excited by the thought of going to Oxford and the challenge of getting into a school that was seen as primarily for wealthy students with distinguished family trees. Although Joanne did well on her entrance examinations, she was not accepted at Oxford.

Joanne and her parents felt that Oxford had rejected her because she was not from an upper-class family and had not attended private school. Whatever the reasons for her rejection, Joanne was humiliated by the failure. The fact that Tutshill was a small town and everyone knew she had failed did not help her feel any better.

Joanne graduated from Wyedean in 1983. She enrolled at Exeter University, a few hours away from her home. Joanne left her days at Wyedean behind without looking back. Despite her extraordinary success later in life, she never returned to the school for a class reunion. To this day, she refuses to wear brown and yellow, the colors of her Wyedean school uniform. For Joanne, college meant a new beginning—even if she still wasn't sure where she wanted to go.

College Rebel

As she entered college, Joanne still dreamed of being a writer. However, she lacked the self-confidence to put her dreams into action. And since she had not told anyone about her plans, no one encouraged her to pursue them.

Peter and Anne Rowling were especially worried about Joanne's apparent lack of ambition. In an effort to get her on the right track, they suggested she study French in college. That way, she could get a job as a bilingual secretary. Since she didn't have a better idea, Joanne reluctantly agreed.

Exeter University was not what Joanne had expected. She had heard that the school was very liberal and allowed students to do pretty much what they wanted. However, Exeter turned out to be very traditional, with many strict rules governing student behavior. Joanne was disappointed, and she felt that studying French, as her parents had suggested, was a big mistake. She later advised young people to learn from her mistake and study what they wanted, not what their parents wanted.

Until she went to college, Joanne had been an excellent student who took school very seriously. At Exeter, however, she often skipped classes and did not complete assignments. Instead, she played guitar, sketched, went to the movies, and visited clubs with her friends. She also spent a great deal of time reading and writing stories. While she was at Exeter, she also began writing her first novel. As usual, she kept her writing private. Only her sister and several close friends even knew what she was doing.

Even though she was not focused on academics, the years at Exeter were important ones. For the first time in her life, Joanne was on her own and had to make her own decisions. Like many students, it took some time for her to settle down and discover what was important.

Although Joanne was sure she should have studied English instead of French, she was good at foreign languages and had no trouble learning French. Best of all, the French program gave her the opportunity to spend a year in Paris, France.

In a Foreign Land

As a foreign language student, during her third year at Exeter Joanne was required to study abroad. So she packed her bags for Paris, where she studied at a university and also taught English as a foreign language to French students.

Joanne loved her experiences in Paris. She enjoyed sightseeing and visiting all the famous places in Paris and the surrounding areas. Most of all, Joanne enjoyed being in a foreign country. The experience of managing everyday life in another land helped her build the self-confidence she lacked. When she returned to Exeter, she was much more sure of herself.

Graduation Day

Joanne had a busy final year at Exeter. She continued to read, play guitar, go to clubs, and study. She also became involved in the production of a French play called *The Agricultural Cosmonaut.* Although Joanne had no desire to appear on stage, she worked hard on the costumes.

During her last year at Exeter, Joanne also fell in love. Her first serious boyfriend was a fellow student at the college. The two remained close for several years. Being in a serious relationship also helped Joanne gain self-confidence.

In 1987, Joanne graduated from Exeter. Her final average was 2.2 out of 4.0 (similar to a grade of C in the United States). Her parents proudly attended the graduation ceremonies. By that time, Anne was in a wheelchair because of the severe effects of her multiple sclerosis.

After graduation, Joanne realized she was really on her own. It was time for her to go out into the world, find a job, and maybe make her dreams come true.

4

DISCOURAGED AND HEARTBROKEN

After graduation, Joanne moved to London to find a job. Her life was about to enter a difficult period, but one that would end in creative triumph.

Off to London

Joanne moved to Clapham, a neighborhood in southwest London. She shared an apartment (or flat, as they're called in England) with several friends from Exeter. Joanne did not have a job, but her parents had an idea of how she could find one. They encouraged Joanne to take classes at a bilingual secretarial school. As she had when her parents suggested studying French at college, Joanne went along with this idea, even though she had no interest in being a secretary.

Joanne completed the course and found secretarial work. However, she soon discovered that she hated being a secretary. Joanne found the jobs boring and uninspiring. She later said that the only good thing about secretarial school was that she learned how to type very quickly—a plus for someone who writes stories.

Like her heroine, writer Jessica Mitford, Joanne longed to do something meaningful with her life. Soon she found a job that she thought would give her that opportunity.

Amnesty International

Soon after she arrived in London, Joanne got a job with an organization called Amnesty International, a group that campaigns for human rights around the world. One of their main goals is to ensure fair trials for political prisoners and the end of human-rights abuses, such as imprisoning someone because of his or her religious or political beliefs.

Joanne was thrilled to get a job as a research assistant with Amnesty International. Her job was to study human-rights abuses in the French-speaking parts of Africa. Joanne was pleased at the thought that she would be working to make the world a better place. At first, she found her job exciting and meaningful.

However, it did not take long for Joanne to realize that her job mostly involved doing clerical work and sitting in an office. Although she would have loved to go to Africa and work directly with the people there, she did not have enough experience to be offered those opportunities. All too soon, her job became just another boring distraction.

Joanne also had trouble making friends with the people she worked with. Although she liked her colleagues, she was not interested in socializing with them. During their lunch hours, many of her coworkers went to lunch together at pubs or cafés. Instead of joining them, Joanne often went off to another café or other place to work on her stories.

Joanne also worked on her stories while she was in the office. Although her bosses never seemed to notice, Joanne often typed her own stories instead of performing her office duties. Other times, she listened to music through headphones instead of the dictation she was supposed to be listening to.

After two years, Joanne tired of the office routine and realized that her job at Amnesty International was never going to amount to anything more than secretarial work. No longer able to stand the boring routine, she resigned.

"The most disorganized person"

Joanne continued to work as a secretary for a variety of different companies. Sometimes she worked temporary jobs, filling in for secretaries who were sick or needed extra help to complete projects. Other times she worked full time in an office.

No matter where she worked, Joanne admitted that she was a terrible secretary. "Anyone who worked with me will tell you that I was the most disorganized person that ever walked the earth," she once told an interviewer. In addition to being disorganized, Joanne found it hard to pay attention to the day-to-day details of her job. She was much more interested in making up stories. More than once, she jotted down notes for stories instead of taking the minutes in meetings. She often spent her lunch hours writing in cafés or typing stories on the office computer.

Obviously, Joanne's bosses were not pleased with her work. She was fired from several jobs. Other times, she quit on her own because she just couldn't stand the work anymore. It seemed like her life was going nowhere.

A Fateful Train Ride

While Joanne was living in London, her college boyfriend had settled in the English city of Manchester, about 150 miles to the northwest. The two resumed their relationship, and Joanne began to spend weekends in Manchester. During these weekends, she visited her boyfriend and looked for an apartment in the city. Then she took the train back to London so she could be back at work first thing Monday morning.

In June 1990, Joanne was on a train heading to King's Cross Station in London (the station where her parents had first met). Suddenly, the train stopped. The conductor announced that the train had a mechanical problem and would not be able to continue its journey for several hours. Joanne had nothing to do besides stare out the window at a field full of cows.

Suddenly, Joanne had a flash of inspiration. In her mind, she saw a dark-haired boy with glasses, green eyes, and a strange lightning-bolt-shaped scar on his forehead. She also had the idea for a school full of young wizards learning their craft.

Joanne was thrilled at her idea. She had never felt such a rush of excitement as she did that day. She looked through her bag to find a pencil and paper to write down her ideas. But for once, she was not carrying anything to write with. Instead, Joanne sat quietly, concentrating on the story unfolding in her mind and committing every detail to memory. By the time the train finally arrived in London, Joanne had the basic outline for the first *Harry Potter* book in her mind. She rushed back to her apartment to write everything down.

Harry continued to fill Joanne's imagination. As she went about her daily routine, his story continued to develop in her mind. Although she had come up with story ideas she liked in the past, she had never had so

Daniel Radcliffe as Harry Potter with his faithful owl, Hedwig (Photofest)

much fun with a story as she was having with the one developing around Harry.

Notes and Dreams

Joanne had already tried to write two adult novels, but she found it difficult to keep the stories going. This time, she decided on a different approach. Instead of starting to write the actual story, Joanne made notes about the characters and their adventures. She wanted to have the whole story completed in her mind before she started writing. She also wanted to know everything about her characters, their homes, and their lives. Soon Joanne had filled several boxes with pages of notes. She soon realized that her story was much too long and complicated to fill a single book. She decided Harry's story would be a seven-book series and that each book would focus on one year of Harry's life at wizard school.

Some people might think that creating a seven-book series is too ambitious for someone who has never published a single story. Joanne did not think that way, however. She wanted to write Harry's story for her own satisfaction and wasn't focused on the details of selling it.

Joanne also did not pay much attention to the type of story she was creating. She did not set out deliberately to write a fantasy novel. Instead, she let the story create itself. It was only after she had come up with the many magical creatures and other fantastic elements of the story that Joanne realized what she was writing. Joanne thought that fantasy was a good way to tell Harry's story. She liked the idea that magical powers would enable Harry to escape his unhappy, ordinary life. "The idea that we could have a child who escapes from the confines of the adult world and goes somewhere where he has power, both literally and metaphorically, really appealed to me," she later explained.

Family Sorrows

Around this time, Joanne decided to move to Manchester to be with her boyfriend. She found a job at the Manchester

Chamber of Commerce, but was soon laid off due to poor performance. Then she worked at Manchester University, but she quickly tired of that job too. She made so little impression at either of these jobs that no one who worked with her even remembers her.

Besides her unfulfilling jobs, Joanne had other pressures during this period. Her mother was losing her long battle with multiple sclerosis. Joanne visited her family over the Christmas holidays in 1990 and then left to spend a few days with friends. Although she knew her mother was very ill, Joanne had lived with her mother's condition for so long that the seriousness of Anne's illness did not really register in her mind. If it had, she probably would have stayed at home rather than going off to visit her friends.

Early in the morning on New Year's Eve, the phone rang. It was Joanne's father. He was calling with the sad news that Anne Rowling had died peacefully at home. Joanne was devastated by the news. She blamed herself for not realizing how sick her mother was and for not staying home with her parents.

Joanne returned home for the funeral and helped her father go through her mother's things. Losing her mother was hard on Joanne, as the two had been very close. Later, she said that if she could speak to her mother again, she would want her to know about the *Harry Potter* books and all the wonderful things that had happened in her life.

Joanne used her writing to ease some of the sorrow and guilt she felt over her mother's death. Like Joanne, Harry had also lost his mother, and Joanne used Harry's story to express her own feelings of loss. In the first *Harry Potter* book, Harry looks into the magical Mirror of Erised (which is "desire" spelled backward) and sees his parents and knows that they are aware of what he is doing. Joanne used this scene to show her own regret for losing her mother and for never telling her about the story that meant so much to her.

Soon after her mother died, Joanne broke up with her boyfriend. The two had been having problems for some time, and finally Joanne realized it was time to end the relationship.

Joanne received another painful blow when she came home to her apartment one night and discovered it had been robbed. All the things that her mother had given her, including many sentimental objects, were gone.

Joanne had had enough. She decided her life needed some dramatic changes. She would no longer work at secretarial jobs and spend most of her time doing work she hated. She wanted a change of scenery too.

One day, Joanne saw a newspaper advertisement from Steve Cassidy, the principal of the Encounter English School in Oporto, Portugal. He was looking for English teachers at his school. Joanne applied for the job. After an interview with Cassidy, she got the job. Joanne packed her things and headed to Portugal.

Life in Portugal

Joanne arrived in Oporto, Portugal, in November 1991. She settled into a four-bedroom apartment provided by Encounter English School. Joanne had two roommates, Aine Kiely and Jill Prewett, who were also teachers at the school. Aine was originally from Ireland, and Jill was from England. Like Joanne, the two women were in their mid-20s. The three young women soon became good friends. Later, Joanne dedicated the third *Harry Potter* book to Aine and Jill.

Oporto is the second largest city in Portugal. About 1.5 million people live in the city and the surrounding area. Oporto is located on the Douro River, near the Atlantic Ocean. The city has been an important port for centuries and is famous for its famous port wines and other tourist attractions.

Joanne settled quickly into her new life. She taught English from 5:00 in the evening to 10:00 at night on weeknights, and she taught on Saturday mornings as well. Most of her students were teenagers who were preparing for school exams. Joanne also taught younger children, as well as adults who wanted to learn English for business purposes or their own enjoyment. However, her primary responsibility was teenagers, and she soon became the head of the program for teens.

Working at night created an ideal schedule for Joanne. She was able to spend mornings and afternoons working on her Harry Potter story. As she had in London, Joanne did most of her writing in cafés. Then she would go to school early to type up her notes before classes began.

Her first few months in Portugal were a very happy time for Joanne. Her writing was going well, she had a job she enjoyed, and she was surrounded by good friends. She enjoyed Portugal too, especially the warm, sunny weather that was so different from England's foggy, rainy climate. The Portuguese people were friendly, and Joanne's students liked her and were doing well.

An Intense Relationship

After an evening of teaching, Joanne and her roommates enjoyed going out at night. They often went to discos and nightclubs to enjoy dancing and listening to music.

One night, Joanne, Aine, and Jill went to a nightclub called Mea Cava. A young Portuguese journalism student named Jorge Arantes saw the women enter and was immediately attracted to Joanne. Jorge and Joanne began to talk and soon discovered they had a lot in common, especially their love of books.

Joanne and Jorge began dating. Soon they were involved in a serious romantic relationship. Not long afterward, they decided to live together. As was the custom in Portugal, the two moved in with Jorge's mother, Marilia Rodrigues. The family lived in a small two-bedroom house.

Although Jorge has publicly said that he supported and encouraged Joanne's writing, the two often had a stormy relationship. There was a lot of jealousy between them. Joanne and Jorge were soon caught up in a cycle of passionate arguments and reconciliations.

Marriage and Motherhood

On August 28, 1992, Jorge asked Joanne to marry him. She agreed, and the wedding took place on October 16, 1992. The wedding was casual and small. Unlike most brides, who wear white, Joanne wore a black dress to get married. She looks serious and not very happy in her wedding photograph. Later, in *Harry Potter and the Prisoner of Azkaban*, a dreaded event takes place on October 16. It seems that Joanne and Jorge's marriage was unhappy from the start.

Soon after they married, Joanne discovered she was pregnant. She continued to teach at Encounter English School during her pregnancy, and she remained friends with Aine and Jill. Jorge worked for Portugal's National

Service. The two continued to fight and spent more time with their friends than with each other.

On July 27, 1993, Joanne gave birth to a baby girl. She named the baby Jessica, after her heroine, Jessica Mitford. Joanne adored being a mother and called Jessica's birth the best moment of her entire life.

Sadly, Jessica's arrival only increased the trouble in Joanne and Jorge's marriage. Joanne was no longer working, which caused significant financial trouble for the family. The stresses of caring for a new baby also hurt the marriage. Joanne was depressed because her husband seemed more interested in his work and his friends than in her. She felt as though she barely existed.

The couple's fights often turned violent. One day, the two argued at a café near the Encounter English School. The fight ended with Jorge pushing Joanne and with Joanne screaming. Then Jorge chased Joanne out of the café and across the street. Joanne locked herself in a classroom. The situation did not calm down until a crowd had gathered and someone called the police.

An End—and a New Beginning

On November 17, 1993, Joanne and Jorge had their worst fight ever. Joanne told Jorge she no longer loved him, and he became so angry that he threw her out of the house. As the neighbors watched, he dragged Joanne outside and slapped her. Then he ran back inside, where Jessica was sleeping, and locked the door.

Joanne went back to the apartment where her friends Aine and Jill were still living. She accepted the fact that her marriage was over, but she refused to leave without her four-month-old daughter. Joanne's friends asked a police officer to go back to the house with Joanne. Jorge agreed to give Jessica to Joanne. Eventually, the couple divorced.

Joanne decided to leave Portugal and return home. She quit her job and, two weeks later, was on a plane to London. Among the items in her suitcases were the notes that would become the *Harry Potter* books.

STRUGGLES AND TRIUMPHS

When Joanne arrived in London, she faced an uncertain future. She had no job, her marriage was over, and she had a baby to care for. With the small amount of money she'd brought with her, Joanne rented an apartment. Then she sat down to plan her future.

Edinburgh

Joanne did not want to stay in London permanently. Her family did not live close by, and most of her friends who lived there were still single and had little in common with her anymore.

Joanne's father, Peter, had remarried less than two years after Anne Rowling died. Joanne has never spoken publicly about her feelings toward her father or his new wife, but it seems that at that time she did not want to rely on him for help. Instead, Joanne turned to her sister, Dianne.

Di had gotten married just a few months earlier to a successful restaurant owner. The young couple was living in Edinburgh, Scotland. Di invited her older sister and niece to stay with her. Joanne agreed. She knew that she and Jessica could not stay with Di and her new husband, Roger, for a long time, but a short visit would give her a chance to figure out what she wanted to do.

Joanne discovered that she liked Edinburgh, the capital of Scotland. She also enjoyed being near her sister, with whom she had always been close. One day, Joanne began telling Di the story of Harry Potter. Di was fascinated and demanded to see what Joanne had written. Joanne gave her the first three chapters and waited anxiously to hear Di's reaction. Di had always been Joanne's closest confidante and listener to her stories. If she didn't like the story, Joanne was sure that it was not worth finishing.

After reading a few pages, Di laughed. She was obviously enjoying Harry and his adventures. Joanne was filled with relief. "It's possible that if she hadn't laughed, I would have set the whole thing to one side," Joanne later said. Di's pleasure gave her the confidence she needed to go on with her writing.

Tough Times

Although Joanne was determined to write her story, she also faced some harsh realities. She had a baby to support and needed to find a job and a place to live.

Joanne's old friend Sean Harris lent her enough money for a deposit on a tiny one-bedroom apartment in Gardens Crescent in Leith, a neighborhood of older buildings in Edinburgh. The apartment was not only very small, it was infested with mice. Joanne was miserable and angry with herself because she could not provide a better place for herself and her daughter to live.

The news got even worse. Although Joanne had a university degree and plenty of teaching experience, she was unable to find a job. Another problem was that she could not work unless she had child care for Jessica, but she could not afford child care unless she had a job.

Reluctantly, Joanne applied for public assistance, or welfare. She was approved for a weekly payment of 69 pounds, a little over $100 at the time. The amount was barely enough to cover food and rent. Sometimes Joanne went to bed hungry because there was not enough food for both herself and her daughter.

Joanne found being on public assistance a humiliating experience. A few months earlier, British Prime Minister John Major had made a speech criticizing single mothers who lived on public assistance. Every time Joanne went to cash her welfare check, she felt like everyone else in line was secretly thinking of her as a lazy woman who expected the government to pay for everything. Her self-respect was at its lowest point.

Joanne applied to the government for money for child care so she could find a job. However, she was turned down. Without a job, Joanne wondered how she could ever make life better for herself and Jessica.

A Fateful Decision

After a great deal of thought, Joanne came up with a plan. She would give herself one year to focus all her energies on finishing her book. Then she would try to get it published. If the book did not find a publisher, Joanne would at least have the satisfaction of knowing she had tried her best. She would make her first serious attempt to publish her writing. After that, she would see about finding a full-time job. This plan allowed Joanne to make the best of a bad situation. It's possible that she saw writing as the only course of action, and that's what finally gave her the courage to become a writer.

Although Joanne was committed to her writing, she found it hard to work in her tiny, shabby apartment. A bigger problem was keeping Jessica entertained while she worked. Joanne soon discovered that she could not get any writing done while Jessica was awake. So she came up with a plan.

Joanne had always enjoyed writing in cafés. Every day, except when the weather was really harsh, Joanne would place baby Jessica in her stroller and walk through the streets of Edinburgh. As soon as Jessica fell asleep, Joanne would duck into a café, order a coffee, and begin to write.

Joanne's favorite café was a place called Nicolson's. Nicolson's was partly owned by Joanne's brother-in-law, so no one complained if she spent hours sitting at a table, nursing a single coffee and scribbling on pieces of paper. In time, Joanne became such a regular customer that the staff got to know her and enjoyed her presence.

Joanne found that she could be amazingly productive writing under pressure. "It's amazing how much you can get done when you know you have very limited time," she later said. "I've probably never been as productive since."

My Friend Harry

As Joanne worked, Harry Potter became more than just a character in a story to her. He became a friend and a champion. Joanne loved leaving her bleak, ordinary world behind and losing herself in the magic of Harry's world. She loved the idea of a character who discovered he had the power to change himself and right wrongs—powers that seemed far beyond Joanne at that point.

Just as Joanne hadn't set out to write a fantasy novel, she also did not deliberately write a book aimed at children. In fact, she wasn't even aware that it was a children's book until later. She always said that she had written *Harry Potter* for herself. It was a story and a set of characters she enjoyed—a sentiment that people all over the world would share.

The *Harry Potter* series begins when an orphaned baby named Harry is given to his aunt and uncle after his parents are killed by an evil wizard named Voldemort. Harry's aunt and uncle, Petunia and Vernon Durlsey, and their spoiled son, Dudley, are horrible to Harry. They force him to sleep in a closet and to wear old, shabby clothes, and they do not allow him to share in the many toys and activities Dudley enjoys. The Dursleys are *Muggles*—humans without magical powers. In fact, the very thought of magic or anything unusual terrifies them.

Everything changes when Harry is 11 years old. He is summoned to attend Hogwarts School of Witchcraft and Wizardry, a secret school that trains children in the magic arts. Until this time, Harry has no idea he is a wizard. He also does not know the true story behind his parents' deaths.

Harry's first days at Hogwarts are difficult, but he is helped by two friends, Ron Weasley and Hermione Granger. The books follow Harry as he adjusts to school life and to his magical powers. Along with the everyday problems of growing up, Harry must learn to control his powers and use them properly. He also takes part in an exciting wizard game called Quidditch. Joanne has described Quidditch as a combination of soccer and basketball. However, the game is played in the air, with students flying around on brooms.

Hanging over all the books like a dark cloud is the presence of an evil wizard named Voldemort. When he kills Harry's parents, Voldemort is unable to kill Harry, leaving the baby with a strange lightning-bolt-shaped scar on his forehead. Their confrontation makes Harry a legend in the wizard world and also weakens Voldemort's powers. Throughout the books, Voldemort tries to regain his strength so he can achieve his dream of ruling the world through his evil powers. It seems inevitable that he and Harry will have one final battle that will resolve their long-standing rivalry. Until then, Harry must learn to use his powers and protect himself from Voldemort until he is strong enough to face the evil wizard.

Joanne had always enjoyed unusual words, and she delighted in making up funny names for the people and places in her novel. She put bits of herself and her friends into the book as well. Harry's friend Ron Weasley, with his turquoise car, is a lot like Joanne's friend Sean Harris. And Hermione Granger, another of Harry's pals, has many of the same qualities as Joanne herself.

Most of all, writing *Harry Potter and the Philosopher's Stone* got Joanne through a very difficult period. She was almost sorry when the book was finished.

The main characters in the Harry Potter books are Ron Weasley, Harry Potter, and Hermione Granger (played here by Rupert Grint, Daniel Radcliffe, and Emma Watson). Joanne finds inspiration for these characters in herself and in people she knows. (Photofest)

The Turning Point

Joanne finished writing the first *Harry Potter* novel in 1995. The manuscript was 80,000 words long—about 200 typed pages. There was no way Joanne could afford to photocopy such a long manuscript. Instead, she saved up the money to buy a cheap typewriter and typed two copies of the story.

Joanne had no idea how to find a publisher for her story. She spent hours in the library, studying guidebooks and lists of publishers and agents. Joanne decided that the best way for her book to get attention was to send it to an agent. The agent, in turn, would send it out to editors and try to find a publisher who would want the book. After researching agents and agencies, Joanne sent the first two chapters of her manuscript to the two agents she felt would be the best fit. She also included a few sketches of Harry and the other characters.

Now that the book was finished, Joanne set about finding a full-time job. She applied to the Scottish Arts Council for a grant, a sum of money that did not have to be paid back. The Arts Council gave Joanne enough money to pay for child care for Jessica. Once she had made arrangements for her daughter's care, Joanne could look for work. She had to obtain a postgraduate certificate of education to become a foreign-language teacher in Scotland. Joanne received a grant from the Scottish Office of Education and

Industry to pay for her schooling and attended a university program to obtain the certificate. Soon afterward, she found a job as a French teacher. Her first job was at the Leith Academy. Later, she taught at another Scottish school, the Moray House Training College.

For the first time in a while, Joanne was feeling optimistic. She had finished her novel and sent it off to agents. She had a full-time job and reliable care for her daughter. Best of all, she was no longer on public assistance and was able to support herself and Jessica.

Joanne eagerly checked the mail, hoping for news from an agent who might want to handle her book. Finally, a letter arrived from Christopher Little, owner of the Christopher Little Literary Agency. When Joanne received the letter, she assumed it was a rejection note. She was stunned and surprised when the letter told her Mr. Little would be pleased to represent her and try to find a publisher for her manuscript. "It was the best letter of my life," Joanne said. "I read it eight times." Then she quickly sent the rest of her manuscript to Little's office.

Christopher Little was actually an odd choice of agent for Joanne because his agency did not represent children's authors. Little's assistant, Bryony Evens, intended to return the manuscript to Joanne without even showing it to her boss. Then she began to glance at the manuscript.

She was intrigued by the drawings Joanne had enclosed and started reading the story. After reading the first few pages, Evens knew the manuscript was a winner. She enjoyed fantasy novels, so the magic and wizardry in the book delighted her. Evens also liked the humor filling the book's pages. She gave the manuscript to Christopher Little and insisted that he read it.

Little was impressed by his assistant's enthusiasm for the book and agreed to take a look at it. He also liked what he read and agreed to become Joanne's agent. He asked Joanne to make some minor revisions, or changes, to her manuscript. Joanne agreed. Once the changes were made, Little and his business partner, Patrick Walsh, offered Joanne a contract.

The contract was a standard agreement that said the agency would be Joanne's only literary agency for five years. After that, the agreement could be renewed every year, as long as both parties agreed. In exchange for representing Joanne's work, the agency would receive 15 percent of any money the book earned in the United Kingdom and 20 percent of any earnings from other countries.

The Search for a Publisher

Christopher Little asked Bryony Evens to send Joanne's manuscript to several different publishers. It was her job to mail the manuscript to editors, along with a cover letter encouraging them to read the manuscript and make an offer to publish it.

Unfortunately, most of the publishers did not share the agency's enthusiasm for the manuscript. *Harry Potter and the Philosopher's Stone* went out to 12 different publishers. Twelve times, the manuscript came back with a polite letter saying, "No thank you." Some editors said the book was too long. Others thought it was too slow-paced or too literary.

Each time Christopher Little told Joanne about another rejection, she was disappointed. However, Little told her not to despair and that the book was so good that a publisher was bound to want it soon. Joanne tried to put *Harry Potter* out of her mind. She stayed busy caring for Jessica and working at her teaching job.

Then Evens sent the manuscript to Bloomsbury Publishing. Bloomsbury was a fairly small publisher that had just started a children's book program. The head of the program was an editor named Barry Cunningham. He was immediately taken by Joanne's story. Cunningham was excited by Joanne's creation and impressed that she had made up such a detailed world and characters.

Cunningham showed the manuscript to other editors at the company. They agreed that the story was a winner. However, Cunningham still had to convince the company's directors, who were more interested in how well the book would sell than in how much fun it was to read.

Cunningham's colleague, Rosemund de la Hay, came up with a clever idea to get the directors to pay attention to the book. She suggested attaching a package of Smarties candy to each copy of the manuscript sent to the directors. In Great Britain, the Smarties Prize is an important award given to the best children's book each year. Whether it was the candy or the story itself, the directors agreed that the book should be published.

Barry Cunningham called Christopher Little and offered an advance of $2,250 against royalties to publish *Harry Potter and the Philosopher's Stone*. This meant that Joanne would get $2,250 up front. As soon as the book earned that much money, she would also receive a small percentage of the price of each book sold.

Little passed the news on to Joanne. She was overjoyed that *Harry Potter* would finally be published. Joanne was so excited that she jumped up and touched the ceiling of her apartment. She later said that nothing since has been as sweet as the moment when she first heard Harry was going to be published. It had been a long, difficult journey.

A Slow Start

Before the book was published, Little asked Joanne an unusual question. Would she mind using a different name as the author of the book? Little explained that girls would read books by male authors but that boys were often reluctant to read books by female authors. He thought it would be easier to sell the book if Joanne used her initials rather than her first name.

Joanne agreed. However, "J. Rowling" sounded too short and plain. Instead, Joanne decided to use "J.K." which stood for Joanne Kathleen. Thus the name J.K. Rowling was born.

Harry Potter and the Philosopher's Stone was published in Great Britain in 1997. Bloomsbury did not expect to sell a lot of the books, so only 500 copies were printed. Joanne did not mind that the book had such a small print run. She only wanted somebody to publish *Harry Potter* so she could go into a bookstore and see it on the shelves. She certainly did not think the book would become a bestseller.

Even though the first *Harry Potter* book was in print, Joanne was not ready to leave the world of Hogwarts behind. As she worked at Leith Academy, she also used her spare time to work on a second book about Harry and his adventures. Because she had already created the characters and plotted the book, the writing went very quickly. In July 1997, only a week after the first book hit the bookstores, Joanne sent the manuscript for *Harry Potter and the Chamber of Secrets* to Christopher Little.

Meanwhile, *Harry Potter and the Philosopher's Stone* was getting good reviews in magazines and newspapers. The *Sunday Times* called the story "very funny, imaginative, and magical" and compared Joanne to the famous British children's author Roald Dahl. A magazine called the *Scotsman* praised Joanne for her "fresh, innovative storytelling."

Stunning News

While *Harry Potter and the Philosopher's Stone* was selling slowly in Great Britain, Christopher Little was also trying to sell foreign rights for the book to be published in other countries. One of the people interested in *Harry Potter and the Philosopher's Stone* was Arthur Levine, the editorial director of Scholastic Books, one of the largest children's book publishers in the United States. Levine had read the book on a long plane trip and was determined to buy the rights for Scholastic. He felt that Harry was a character who would appeal to many readers, since everyone had experienced feelings of being unappreciated and wishing he or she had the power to change everything.

Several other publishers were interested in *Harry Potter* besides Levine. The book went to auction. Each publisher announced how much money he or she was willing to spend and waited to see if another publisher topped that bid. As Levine watched, the bidding rose to $50,000. Then it went even higher, to $60,000 and $70,000. Levine began to get nervous. He had never offered so much money for a children's book. But he was sure *Harry Potter* would become a classic and would be worth every penny.

Finally, Levine made the final bid for *Harry Potter*—a stunning $105,000. He won the auction. Harry was going to America, and Scholastic would be his publisher.

Christopher Little called Joanne with the news. At first she couldn't believe her ears. She didn't know that books were auctioned and could not figure out what Little was talking about. When he told her that Scholastic had bought United States rights to the book for more than $100,000, Joanne almost went into shock. "This was like being catapulted into fairyland," she later said.

Later that night, Arthur Levine called Joanne, and the two had a long talk. Levine understood the pressures Joanne was suddenly facing and told her not to be frightened. But Joanne was very frightened. Suddenly, she was no longer a person who had written a book that sold a few thousand copies. She was about to become a world-famous—and very wealthy—author.

6

WILD ABOUT HARRY

Very few children's books had ever sold for more than $100,000. When the media heard about the *Harry Potter* auction, Joanne and Harry both became big news. Suddenly, everyone wanted to talk to Joanne. Newspapers, magazines, and radio and television stations called her, asking for an interview or at least a few comments. Joanne's picture was in the newspapers. People everywhere were talking about what Scholastic had done.

Many people in the publishing industry thought that Arthur Levine had made a big mistake. Even if *Harry Potter* was as good as he thought it was, it seemed very unlikely that a children's book could sell enough copies to justify such a huge advance. However, Levine and Christopher Little had great faith in Joanne's book. They told her not to worry.

However, Joanne could not help worrying. Before Scholastic had bought the United States rights, she had been content to think that her book would sell a few thousand copies. Now, everything had changed. There was a great deal of pressure on her to succeed.

The sale of her book to an American publisher also meant that Joanne could leave her teaching job at Leith Academy. Although the school offered her a new contract, Joanne turned it down. She was finally in a position to be a full-time author.

In the Public Eye

Joanne was a shy person, but she realized that she had to make public appearances in order to sell her book. However, she worried that her new popularity and the amount of time she would have to spend on publicity would seriously cut into the time she devoted to writing.

Joanne was featured on television shows and in newspaper and magazine articles. Reporters told and retold the story of how she came to write the books. Joanne's face was on magazine covers and on the front page of newspapers. It was all a bit overwhelming for the shy schoolteacher.

Joanne also became annoyed at the way the media portrayed her. Many articles described her as an unemployed single mother who received public assistance and was liv-

Although Joanne was initially overwhelmed by her sudden fame, she has always loved to meet her many fans. Here she greets a crowd at London's Royal Albert Hall. (Associated Press)

ing in desperate circumstances. The truth was that Joanne was an educated, hard-working woman who'd had a job and had been off public assistance for some time before the first *Harry Potter* book was published.

The media also tended to exaggerate the facts of Joanne's life. One report said she wrote in cafés because her apartment had no heat. Joanne was angry at the thought that people believed she would live in an unheated apartment, which could have serious health consequences for her daughter. The media routinely exaggerated the amount of the advance Joanne received from Scholastic. One story in London's *Sunday Times* hinted that she had actually received $500,000.

Joanne was also hurt when her ex-husband, Jorge Arantes, sold his story to a British newspaper. Joanne insisted that some of the things he said—including hints that he had helped Joanne write *Harry Potter*—were completely untrue.

Joanne was fiercely protective of her daughter, Jessica. She wanted to shield Jessica from publicity and became angry if a magazine or newspaper published photos of the child. Joanne even filed a complaint with the British government after a magazine published photos of her and Jessica on the beach during a vacation.

Super Sales

Despite her dislike of publicity, Joanne could not deny that it helped sales of her book. Scholastic ordered a 50,000-copy print run for *Harry Potter and the Sorcerer's Stone*, and the book sold out soon after it was published in August 1998. The book became a number-one best-seller in the United States. By the end of 1998, Scholastic had gone back to press seven times, and more than 190,000 books were in print in the United States.

Harry Potter was doing very well in Great Britain too. By the end of 1997, the book had won the Smarties Prize. It also won the Federation of Children's Books Group Award and was named the British Book Awards Children's Book of the Year. After one year in print, British sales of *Harry Potter and the Philosopher's Stone* totaled more than 70,000 copies.

The Harry Potter books have set many records in the book industry. Here an Amazon.com employee prepares copies of Harry Potter and the Order of the Phoenix *for the book's release date.* (Associated Press)

Changes for America

Scholastic asked Joanne to make some changes for the American edition of the book. The most important change was the title. Executives at Scholastic did not think that American children would respond well to the "Philosopher's Stone" in the title. Instead, they wanted to use the more familiar and exciting term "Sorcerer's Stone."

Joanne was not happy about this revision and tried to change the executives' minds. However, in the end, she agreed that they knew the American audience better than she did. The book was published in the United States as *Harry Potter and the Sorcerer's Stone.*

Joanne was also asked to change some British expressions for the American edition. For example, Ron Weasley wears a *jumper* in the British edition. *Jumper* is the British word for sweater. However, in the United States, a jumper is a kind of dress. Joanne did not want American readers to think that Ron was wearing a dress, so she quickly agreed to this change. However, she did not want to change the British word *mum* to *mom*. Scholastic agreed, and mum remained in the American edition.

Harry Potter and the Chamber of Secrets

In the middle of all this attention about the first *Harry Potter* book, Joanne needed to focus on the second book in the series. She had already given the manuscript for *Harry*

Potter and the Chamber of Secrets to Barry Cunningham at Bloomsbury by the time the first book became a best-seller. Now Joanne began to worry that the second book was not as good as the first one. This is a common fear for best-selling authors, and it put even more pressure on Joanne.

Joanne was so worried that she asked Bloomsbury to return the manuscript of the second book to her. She kept the book for six weeks, struggling to make changes she felt would make the book better. She later said this was the only time in her life she had suffered from writer's block, the inability to write. Finally, Joanne decided the manuscript was good enough and sent it back to Bloomsbury.

During this hectic period, Joanne also decided to move out of her tiny apartment in Leith. With some of the money Scholastic had paid her, she bought a small house on Hazelbank Terrace. For the first time, Jessica had her own bedroom. Joanne also had enough space to use one room as an office. It was a relief for her not to have to worry about money. For the first time, she did not have to agonize over whether she could afford a new pair of shoes for Jessica. She even bought a computer. However, she still enjoyed writing her stories by hand in Edinburgh's cafés.

Joanne and Jessica loved their new neighborhood. The area was full of families with young children and was within walking distance of an excellent school for Jessica. Joanne, who had never learned to drive, was also pleased that she could walk to her sister's house from her new home.

Harry Potter and the Chamber of Secrets was published in Great Britain in July 1998. It immediately rose to the top of the best-seller lists, outselling many adult titles. Scholastic had planned to publish the book in September, but Joanne's American fans could not wait that long. As soon as they found out the book was already available in Great Britain, many began ordering copies over the Internet. Scholastic quickly rushed *Harry Potter and the Chamber of Secrets* into print so it would not lose sales.

Joanne was surprised and a bit amused by the success of her work. She had not expected the book to do so well in the United States, because the story was set in England and featured many British aspects. Her explanations for the book's success were that children told one another how much they enjoyed it and that a good book will sell, no matter what.

Harry Potter and the Prisoner of Azkaban

The first two *Harry Potter* books were so successful that publishers no longer worried about sales. Scholastic and Bloomsbury both signed contracts with Joanne to complete the seven-book series she had always imagined.

Joanne was happy to be able to continue writing about Harry with the security that the books would be published. However, she still felt the pressure to perform, since it seemed that the whole world was waiting for her every word. To calm herself and make sure the remaining books would go smoothly, Joanne sat down and outlined the remaining five books. For Joanne, this was a labor of love, for she truly enjoyed creating Harry's world and writing his adventures.

Although Joanne outlined the major plot developments of the series, she did not figure out many of the books' smaller details ahead of time. Joanne preferred to let her imagination come up with creative solutions as she worked on the books. This approach also allowed her characters the freedom to do and say things in a more natural, unscripted way and to leave some surprises for Joanne to come up with as she actually wrote the series.

Joanne's third book was *Harry Potter and the Prisoner of Azkaban.* As she worked on the book, she was constantly distracted by the demands of publicity. Some of these demands, such as giving interviews to the media, were boring and sometimes frustrating. However, Joanne did, and still does, enjoy book signings and school visits. She genuinely loves children and enjoys meeting them and sharing her stories with them. Joanne especially enjoys when children quote parts of her book to her.

A Tidal Wave of Sales

Harry Potter and the Prisoner of Azkaban was published in Great Britain on July 8, 1999. Bloomsbury Publishing told bookstores not to start selling the book until 3:45 in the afternoon. That was the time when students were dismissed from school. Bloomsbury made this request because it was afraid students would skip school in order to be the first to buy the book.

As soon as 3:45 rolled around, bookstores were overwhelmed by a tidal wave of buyers. Children—and adults too—lined up to purchase the latest *Harry Potter* book. The stores could barely keep up with demand. Within two weeks, the book had sold more than 270,000 copies and gone through 10 printings.

Once again, readers in the United States had to wait for the American edition, which had a later publication date than the British version. As they had with the second book, many people in the United States bought copies of the British book online. To prevent this from happening again, Arthur Levine decided that all future *Harry Potter* books would be published on the same date in Great Britain and the United States.

An American Tour

Joanne knew she was popular in America, but she had no idea how popular until 1999. That October, she came to the United States to do book signings and other public appearances. Joanne had been to the United States once before and read her book before a small number of fans. This time, she was stunned when thousands of people showed up at book signings.

Joanne said she felt a bit like a rock star during the 1999 American tour. She could hardly believe it when she saw fans lined up for blocks outside bookstores where she was going to sign books. At one bookstore in Boston, she signed 1,400 books in one day. For the first time, Joanne realized how many children really loved Harry and his world. Later, she would return to the United States and also tour Canada. During these tours, she often spoke at stadiums in front of 10,000 or more excited fans. As a former teacher, Joanne was used to speaking in front of groups. However, she found it strange to be speaking in front of such huge crowds. It was hard for her to believe that so many people were interested in seeing her and hearing her speak. Joanne also found it somewhat terrifying to make appearances in front of these large audiences. However, she was moved to see so many people—especially children—who loved Harry and his world so much. She loved the idea that her story had touched so many lives.

Press tours could be stressful in other ways as well. During one stop on a tour, Joanne had trouble checking out of her hotel because of problems with the computerized reservation system. After arguing with the manager and finally resolving the problem, Joanne rushed off to her appearance in a taxi, only to discover that she had left her purse at the hotel. Adding to the stress, all these problems had made her late for her book-signing appearance. Joanne was so frustrated she burst into tears. But these problems were few and far between, and Joanne managed to enjoy her celebrity status most of the time.

Troubles with Harry

After Joanne came home from the United States, she started writing the fourth book in the series, *Harry Potter and the Goblet of Fire.* Writing this book turned out to be harder than she thought. Although the first three books had been long and complicated, the fourth book was even more so. Joanne had to be careful not to confuse her readers with the many characters and situations. It was even hard for her to keep the pieces of the puzzle together. Several times, Joanne discovered mistakes or holes in the plot. Many scenes had to be rewritten for the book to make sense and read well. Joanne revised her books heavily as she went along to make sure the story worked. She usually did not show her work to anyone until she submitted it to her agent and then to her publisher.

Joanne realized that she was not going to meet her deadline for delivering the manuscript to the publisher. As the media speculated that she had writer's block or other reasons for the delay, Joanne kept working 10-hour days to finish the book. Finally, she delivered the manuscript for the fourth book to Bloomsbury two months late.

A Cloak of Secrecy

Both Joanne and her publishers knew that people could not wait to find out what happened in *Harry Potter and the Goblet of Fire*. To prevent any parts of the story from leaking out, everything about the book was kept a secret. Even the title was hidden from the media, and the book was simply known as *Harry Potter IV*. Joanne's editor at Bloomsbury even locked the manuscript in a bank vault to keep it hidden from view.

In spite of all efforts, the cover picture and the title of the book did appear in the media on June 26, about two weeks before the book's official release date. A few days later, a clerk at a store in Virginia mistakenly sold a copy of the book to a young customer.

Party Time!

In the end, the leaks did not hurt sales of the book at all. On July 8, thousands of children lined up at bookstores around the world to buy the book. Some stores even put

Fans line up by the thousands to attend Joanne's book signings. (Associated Press)

the book on sale at the stroke of midnight and hosted parties. Children and their parents were encouraged to go to stores dressed up as their favorite characters. Booksellers prepared refreshments based on food and drink from the books and hosted trivia contests and other games based on the series.

Joanne joined in on the fun too. To promote the book, Bloomsbury sent her on a short tour of Great Britain. Joanne made the trip on an old steam train labeled "Hogwarts Express." Like the train that takes Harry and his classmates to school in the books, Joanne's train left

King's Cross Station in London at 11:00 in the morning. Joanne arrived at the station in a turquoise car like the one in her books.

Controversy and Anger

Although Harry Potter has millions of fans around the world, not everyone is happy with the books. Soon after the first book became popular, a number of conservative religious groups became concerned with the story. These groups insisted that the books promoted witchcraft, devil worship, and other rituals that defied the Christian faith.

Members of these groups wrote letters to newspapers and magazines. Some tried to get the books removed from classrooms and libraries. In 2001, a minister in New Mexico even burned copies of the *Harry Potter* books in front of his congregation.

Joanne was angry and upset at this reaction to her books. In several interviews, she insisted that the *Harry Potter* series did not encourage or teach readers to become witches or wizards. She was especially upset at people who claimed the books were evil. Joanne insisted that anyone who had read the books could clearly see that good always triumphed over evil and that there was no devil worship or other elements that glamorized evil.

Many authors have had their books banned or censored, and many people are disturbed by efforts to ban books.

The *Harry Potter* series has strong defenders, and several organizations have been formed to fight against any attempts to ban the series. Groups such as Muggles for Harry Potter have received support from the American Booksellers Foundation for Free Expression, the Association of American Publishers, and other national organizations. The *Harry Potter* books have also found some supporters among conservative Christians, who point out that the series has strong moral values and does not violate Christian ideals.

Although some teachers might have questioned the use of magic in the *Harry Potter* books, most were thrilled at the way the books encouraged children to read. Some of the series' biggest fans were children who had not been interested in reading before. Reading the *Harry Potter* novels changed that. Even reluctant readers became caught up in Harry's adventures and didn't find it hard to get through a book that was several hundred pages long. And once they had read the *Harry Potter* books, these children were eager to read other fantasies. *Harry Potter* opened the door to a love of books for children around the world. The books were used in classroom discussions and assigned to book clubs in schools and libraries. College courses were developed around the books as well. Literary guides were even published to help readers understand the complex storylines and themes.

Censorship was not the only conflict Joanne faced after the *Harry Potter* books became popular. In 1984, an American author named Nancy Stouffer published a children's book called *Legend of Rah and the Muggles*, which became the first book in a series. After the *Harry Potter* books came out, Stouffer and her friends noticed many similarities between her books and Joanne's. Stouffer had created a character named Larry Potter, and he has black hair and round eyeglasses, just like Harry does. Stouffer also had characters named Muggles.

Joanne receives an award from Spain's Crown Prince Felipe for her works, which have linked continents and generations. (Landov)

Stouffer claimed that Joanne had plagiarized, or stolen the ideas from her books. Her claims received a lot of publicity, but Joanne denied ever reading Stouffer's books or stealing ideas from them. Joanne, Scholastic Books, and Time Warner Entertainment Company filed a lawsuit against Stouffer demanding that she stop accusing Joanne of stealing the term Muggles or violating Stouffer's copyright. Stouffer then filed her own lawsuit against Joanne and the other defendants. In 2002, a judge found in Joanne's favor, and Stouffer's suit was dismissed.

Books for Charity

The *Harry Potter* books made a great deal of money for Joanne, and she was eager to share her wealth with others who were not as fortunate. Although she now had a comfortable life, she would never forget the difficult days when she struggled with poverty and unemployment.

Joanne was especially sympathetic to single mothers who relied on public assistance to raise their children. In 2000, she donated $725,000 to the National Council for One Parent Families and also served as that charity's spokesperson.

In 2001, Joanne wrote two short books to accompany the *Harry Potter* series. These books were *Quidditch through the Ages* and *Fantastic Beasts and Where to Find*

Them. Once again, Joanne indulged her love of unusual names and published these books under the pen names Kennilworthy Whisp and Newt Scamander. The two books are not novels but instead serve as references that provide details about elements of Harry Potter's world: Quidditch is a sporting event that plays an important role in the *Harry Potter* novels, and unusual creatures appear throughout the books. The books also appear on the required reading list for students at Hogwarts. Joanne donated all the profits from these books to a charity called Comic Relief U.K., which helps underprivileged children and their families.

A Break in the Schedule

Joanne had been publishing a new *Harry Potter* novel every year since 1997. However, *Quidditch through the Ages* and *Fantastic Beasts and Where to Find Them* were the only books she published in 2001.

Fans wondered if Joanne was having trouble writing the fifth book in the series. The media picked up on their concern, and reports appeared claiming that Joanne was suffering from writer's block or other difficulties.

In reality, Joanne just wanted to slow down. She was working on the fifth book and still enjoyed writing more than anything else. However, she had been writing, traveling, and doing publicity at a furious pace for almost five years, and she knew that her writing would suffer as a result of too much pressure.

In 2002, *Harry Potter and the Order of the Phoenix* was finally published. The fifth book in the series was the longest one, at 896 pages, but readers did not mind. Once again, bookstores held parties and fans lined up for hours to buy the book. During that summer, it was not unusual to see children and adults around the world curled up with a copy of the latest *Harry Potter* adventure.

7

A WHOLE NEW WORLD

Joanne's books had captivated readers around the world. It wasn't long before Hollywood took note. In 2001, *Harry Potter* became more than a book. It was turned into a movie.

The Studios Come Calling

Joanne was first approached by movie studios in 1997, after *Harry Potter and the Philosopher's Stone* was published in Great Britain. Two British studios and two American studios asked Joanne's agent, Christopher Little, for the right to film the book.

Joanne and Little both said no. Joanne was focused on writing the books and felt it was too early to think about turning them into movies. Also, Joanne loved movies but knew that many books are changed drastically in their film versions. She did not want to lose control of her characters.

By 1999, the *Harry Potter* series was well established. Once again, Christopher Little received offers from film companies. This time, he and Joanne were ready to make a deal.

Joanne had some rules that she wanted the studios to follow. First of all, she did not want Harry Potter to be turned into a cartoon. The movie had to be a live-action film. She also insisted that the filmmakers not leave out any characters or introduce new ones and that they not have the characters do things they never do in the books. It was very important to Joanne that no one take her characters and make them do things she did not want them to do.

An American company called Warner Brothers agreed to Joanne's rules and said that she could have creative input on the films. In 1999, Joanne signed with Warner Brothers for about $1 million.

Mixed Reactions

Not everyone was happy when word of a *Harry Potter* movie came out. Some fans were thrilled at the idea of seeing their hero and his adventures brought to life on the big screen. Other fans resented the idea of turning the book into a movie. Many of these fans already had a clear picture in their minds of Harry, his friends and enemies, and the aspects of life at Hogwarts. They feared that a movie version would not get the story right and might even ruin their images of the books.

Important Choices

Warner Brothers knew that it had to find the right director to bring the books to life and keep Harry's fans satisfied. At first, noted director Steven Spielberg was involved in the movie, but later he passed on the project. After interviewing several different directors, Warner Brothers settled on director Chris Columbus.

At first, Columbus seemed an odd choice to direct a *Harry Potter* movie. Although he was a successful director who had worked with Spielberg earlier in his career, Columbus was known more for comedies such as *Home Alone* and *Mrs. Doubtfire*. However, Columbus had worked with many children in his movies and was good at bringing the magic of childhood to life on screen.

Warner Brothers also hired a screenwriter to create a script from Joanne's novel. Steve Kloves, a screenwriter not known for fantasy films, got the job. Kloves turned out to be a good choice, however, because he wisely focused on the characters and their stories, not just on the magical events going on around them.

Finally, actors and actresses had to be cast in the film. After many auditions, the leading roles were given to a group of relatively unknown British actors. Daniel Radcliffe

Joanne with the stars of Harry Potter and the Chamber of Secrets (Getty Images)

would play Harry, Rupert Grint would play Ron, and Emma Watson would take on the role of Hermione. The major adult roles were played by noted actors John Cleese, Richard Harris, Maggie Smith, and Robbie Coltrane. Joanne was able to make suggestions about some of the actors cast. She also viewed the screen tests of the children who auditioned. In the end, she was pleased with the cast and wished them "as much fun acting the first year at Hogwarts as I had writing it."

People were busy behind the scenes as well. Set designers had the difficult task of recreating the amazingly complicated world of Hogwarts in the real world. Special-effects artists worked on showing Harry and his classmates flying on broomsticks as they played the game of Quidditch. Special effects were also needed to show some of the unique characters in the film, including a three-headed dog, many monsters, and other magical creatures.

Another Hit

The film *Harry Potter and the Sorcerer's Stone* came out on November 2, 2001. Most fans were delighted. They were pleased that the film version stayed true to the books and did not change or cheapen the characters or the story. Critics enjoyed the movie as well, although some complained that it followed the book too closely. In the end, Joanne was more concerned that her fans were happy with the movie than with what critics had to say. She herself thought the film had done a great job of bringing her story to life.

Harry Potter and the Sorcerer's Stone became the number-one film in the United States that year. It broke box office records during its first few days of release, earning more than $93 million. In just two months, the movie made more than $286 million in the United States. The movie broke records in Great Britain as well.

Along with the release of the movie came a rush of merchandising tie-ins. Suddenly, Harry's face was appearing on everything from toys to soda bottles to clothes. Joanne had been reluctant to license Harry's image for merchandise, although she realized this was a necessary part of the movie's promotion. Still, she tried to limit the type of merchandise and made sure that Harry did not appear on anything truly cheap or embarrassing.

Personal Happiness

The year 2001 was an exciting time in Joanne's personal life as well as in her professional one. Earlier, she had bought an estate called Killiechassie House in the Scottish countryside. On the estate, on December 26, 2001, Joanne married for the second time. Her new husband was Dr. Neil Murray. The ceremony was very small, with only 15 people attending. Among the guests were Joanne's daughter, sister, father, and stepmother, as well as her new husband's parents and sister.

Joanne also bought a house in London, so she could be closer to her publisher and her friends there. And she continued giving generously to charity. In 2001, she began doing charity work for Scotland's MS Society and often spoke of her mother's 10-year battle with the disease. Joanne also continued her work for the National Council of One Parent Families and still works for the

Joanne and her husband, Neil Murray (Getty Images)

Maggies Centers in Edinburgh, which help cancer patients and their families.

The year 2003 brought more happiness into Joanne's life. That year, Joanne and Neil's son, David Gordon Murray, was born. Despite her fame, Joanne was determined to live a normal life with her family. She did her own shopping, valued being able to walk down the street unnoticed, and claimed that her life was not that interesting. Most of all,

Joanne treasured the time she spent with her family. She was especially insistent that her children be left alone and not photographed or interviewed by the media. Joanne felt that there was no reason Jessica and David's lives should be disrupted just because their mother was a famous author.

A Bright Future

By 2003, Joanne had published five of the seven books in the *Harry Potter* series. She has seen her idea grow from a pile of handwritten papers to a series of fat books beloved by readers all over the world. She has also seen Harry and his world brought to the big screen, with two hit movies and more to come.

Just how big is *Harry Potter?* Scholastic announced that by the end of 2003, the series had a total of 96 million books in print in the United States alone and 254 million copies around the world. The books have been translated into 61 languages. The first two movies are among the 25 highest grossing films of all time, and the third film, *Harry Potter and the Prisoner of Azkaban,* released in 2004, was also a smashing success. There are *Harry Potter* websites that discuss every aspect of the books and allow fans from around the world to communicate with each other. Conventions, or gatherings of *Harry Potter* fans, are held around the world as well. All of this has made Joanne one of the richest women in the world. Some media reports say she is the richest woman in Great Britain and even has more money the Queen Elizabeth II.

The series owes much of its success to the fact that it appeals to both children and adults. Although the books feature young people as the main characters, they are complex enough to keep adults entertained as well. Also, the fantasy setting is one that appeals to a wide spectrum of

Joanne meets Queen Elizabeth II of England during a reception at Buckingham Palace to honor Britain's women achievers. (Getty Images)

ages. The main reason for the books' wide appeal, however, lies in their timeless themes. The series works on several different levels. Along with being a rollicking adventure full of danger, excitement, humor, and fascinating characters, the *Harry Potter* novels focus on themes such as good versus evil and the powerless discovering hidden strengths that can change their lives. These are themes that appeal to most people, no matter what their ages.

Joanne continues to write the final two *Harry Potter* books. In recent years, she has made fewer pubic appearances. Keeping a low profile allows her to focus on her writing and her family.

Although she can now afford several beautiful homes, computers, and other luxuries she never could have dreamed of during those early days in Edinburgh, Joanne still follows the same writing routine she did in the early days of writing the series. She has said that cafés and writing are strongly linked in her mind, so she still does much of her work while sipping coffee in several favorite cafés. She also still writes the first drafts of all of her books by hand because she likes the sound and feel of shuffling papers. Later, Joanne types her work on a computer at home, but her first drafts are always done by hand.

Since *Harry Potter* has become a global phenomenon, reviewers, fans, and critics have produced thousands of

Joanne's remarkable story is proof that success can be achieved through imagination and determination. (Landov)

words commenting on the novels. Although some writers might be affected by these comments and even change their stories because of them, Joanne is secure enough in her story to avoid that reaction. She has had the entire *Harry Potter* series plotted and outlined for years and has not allowed public criticism or pressure to change her mind. The stories are written the way she originally conceived them.

When the *Harry Potter* series is finally finished, Joanne will face a huge void in her life. For the first time in more than 10 years, she will not have a Harry story to write down. Joanne has said that once the seventh book is published, Harry will leave Hogwarts and the series will be complete.

Joanne knows that she will probably never write anything as popular as the *Harry Potter* books and that she will forever be known as "the woman who wrote *Harry Potter*." This is fine with her, since she put her heart and soul into the books, and they are very dear to her. She jokes that after she finishes the series, she might write an adult novel about some obscure topic that no one will care about. The truth is that Joanne doesn't know yet what she will do once the *Harry Potter* series is complete.

Most authors—especially authors of children's books— never reach the heights of success that Joanne Rowling has. It is not even that common for an unknown author to submit a manuscript unsolicited and have it published at all. Joanne's success has fueled the dreams of many other writers. Her creations show that with a brilliant imagination and the will to succeed, even the most ordinary person can achieve amazing success.

TIME LINE

1965   Joanne Kathleen Rowling is born on July 31 in Yate, England

1967   Joanne's sister, Dianne, is born

1971   The Rowlings move to Winterbourne; Joanne begins writing stories

1974   The Rowlings move to Church Cottage in Tutshill

1976   Graduates from Tutshill Primary School and begins Wyedean Preparatory School

1980   Joanne's mother is diagnosed with multiple sclerosis

1983   Graduates from Wyedean and enrolls at Exeter University

1985   Spends a semester in Paris, France

1987   Graduates from Exeter and begins working at office jobs in London

1990   Comes up with the idea for the *Harry Potter* books while stranded on a train; Joanne's mother, Anne Rowling, dies

1991   Moves to Oporto, Portugal, to teach English; meets Jorge Arantes

1992   Marries Jorge Arantes

1993   Gives birth to daughter Jessica; separates from Arantes; moves to Edinburgh, Scotland

1994   Receives public assistance while writing the first *Harry Potter* book

1995   Completes *Harry Potter and the Philosopher's Stone* and submits it to agents; obtains teaching certificate and begins working full time

1996   *Harry Potter and the Philosopher's Stone* is accepted by the Christopher Little Literary Agency; Bloomsbury Publishers agrees to publish the book

1997   *Harry Potter and the Philosopher's Stone* is published in Great Britain; Joanne completes *Harry Potter and the Chamber of Secrets*

1998   Scholastic Books pays more than $100,000 for U.S. rights to publish *Harry Potter and the Sorcerer's Stone*; the book is published in the United States; Joanne becomes a worldwide celebrity; *Harry Potter*

and the Chamber of Secrets is published in Great Britain

1999   *Harry Potter and the Prisoner of Azkaban* is published in the United States and Great Britain; Joanne holds the top three positions on the *New York Times* best seller list

2000   *Harry Potter and the Goblet of Fire* is published in the United States and Great Britain and becomes the fastest selling book of all time

2001   *Quidditch through the Ages* and *Fantastic Beasts and Where to Find Them* are published; the movie version of *Harry Potter and the Sorcerer's Stone* is released and becomes the number-one movie of the year; receives the Order of the British Empire from Queen Elizabeth II; marries Dr. Neil Murray

2002   *Harry Potter and the Order of the Phoenix* is published; the movie version of *Harry Potter and the Chamber of Secrets* is released

2003   Son David Gordon Murray is born

HOW TO BECOME A WRITER

THE JOB

Writers work in the field of communications. They deal with the written word, whether it is destined for the printed page, broadcast, computer screen, or live theater. The nature of their work is as varied as the materials they produce: books, magazines, trade journals, newspapers, technical reports, company newsletters and other publications, advertisements, speeches, scripts for motion picture and stage productions, and scripts for radio and television broadcasts. Writers develop ideas and write for all media.

Prose writers for newspapers, magazines, and books share many of the same duties. First they come up with an idea for an article or book from their own interests or are assigned a topic by an editor. The topic is of relevance to the particular publication; for example, a writer for a magazine on parenting may be assigned an article on car seat safety. Then writers begin gathering as much information as possible about the subject through library research, interviews, the Internet, observation, and other methods. They keep extensive notes from which they will draw material for their project. Once the material has been organized and arranged in logical sequence, writers prepare a written outline. The process of developing a piece of writing is exciting, although it can also involve detailed and solitary work. After researching an idea, a writer might discover that a different perspective or related topic would be more effective, entertaining, or marketable.

When working on an assignment, writers often submit their outlines to a literary agent, an editor, or a publishing company representative for approval. Then they write a first draft of the manuscript, trying to put the material into words that will have the desired effect on their audience. They rewrite and polish sections of the material as they proceed, always searching for just the right way of imparting information or expressing an idea or opinion. A manuscript may be reviewed, corrected, and revised numerous times before a final copy is submitted. Even after that, an editor may request additional changes.

Writers for newspapers, magazines, or books often specialize in their subject matter. Some writers might have an educational background that allows them to give critical interpretations or analyses. For example, a health or science writer for a newspaper typically has a degree in biology and can interpret new ideas in the field for the average reader.

Columnists or *commentators* analyze news and social issues. They write about events from the standpoint of their own experience or opinion. *Critics* review literary, musical, or artistic works and performances. *Editorial writers* write on topics of public interest, and their comments, consistent with the viewpoints and policies of their employers, are intended to stimulate or mold public opinion. *Newswriters* work for newspapers, radio, or TV news departments, writing news stories from notes supplied by reporters or wire services.

Corporate writers and writers for nonprofit organizations have a wide variety of responsibilities. These writers may work in such places as a large insurance corporation or a small nonprofit religious group, where they may be required to write news releases, annual reports, speeches for the company head, or public relations materials. Typically, they are assigned a topic with length requirements for a given project. They may receive raw research materials, such as statistics, and they are expected to conduct additional research, including personal interviews. These writers must be able to write quickly and accurately on short deadlines, while also working with people whose primary job is not in the communications field. The written work is submitted to a supervisor, and often a legal department, for approval; rewrites are a normal part of this job.

Copywriters write copy primarily designed to sell goods and services. Their work appears as advertisements in newspapers, magazines, and other publications or as commercials on radio and television broadcasts. Sales and marketing representatives first provide information on the product and help determine the style and length of the copy. The copywriters conduct additional research and interviews; to formulate an effective approach, they study advertising trends and review surveys of consumer preferences. Armed with this information, copywriters write a draft that is submitted to the account executive and the client for approval. The copy is often returned for correction and revision until everyone involved is satisfied. Copywriters, like corporate writers, may also write articles, bulletins, news releases, sales letters, speeches, and other related informative and promotional material. Many copywriters are employed in advertising agencies. They also may work for public relations firms or in communications departments of large companies.

Technical writers can be divided into two main groups: those who convert technical information into material for the general public and those who convey technical information among professionals. Technical writers in the first group may prepare service manuals or handbooks, instruction or repair booklets, or sales literature or brochures; those in the second group may write grant proposals, research reports, contract specifications, or research abstracts.

Screenwriters prepare scripts for motion pictures or television. They select, or are assigned, a subject, conduct research, write and submit a plot outline and narrative synopsis (treatment), and confer with the producer and/or director about possible revisions. Screenwriters may adapt books or plays for film and television dramatizations. They often collaborate with other screenwriters and may specialize in a particular type of script or writing.

Playwrights do similar writing for the stage. They write dialogue and describe action for plays that may be tragedies, comedies, or dramas, with themes sometimes adapted from fictional, historical, or narrative sources. Playwrights combine the elements of action, conflict, purpose, and resolution to depict events from real or imaginary life. They often make revisions even while the play is in rehearsal.

Continuity writers prepare the material read by radio and television announcers to introduce or connect various parts of their programs.

Novelists and *short story writers* create stories that may be published in books, magazines, or literary journals. They take incidents from their own lives, from news events, or from their imaginations and create characters, settings, actions, and resolutions. *Poets* create narrative, dramatic, or lyric poetry for books, magazines, or other publications, as well as for special events such as commemorations. These writers may work with literary agents or editors who help guide them through the writing process, which includes research of the subject matter and an understanding of the intended audience. Many universities and colleges offer graduate degrees in creative writing. In these programs, students work intensively with published writers to learn the art of storytelling.

Writers can be employed either as in-house staff or as freelancers. Pay varies according to experience and the position, but freelancers must provide their own office space and equipment such as computers and fax machines. Freelancers also are responsible for keeping tax records, sending out invoices, negotiating contracts, and providing their own health insurance.

REQUIREMENTS

High School

While in high school, build a broad educational foundation by taking courses in English, literature, foreign languages, general science, social studies, computer science, and typing. The ability to type is almost a requisite for all positions in the communications field, as is familiarity with computers.

Postsecondary Training

Competition for writing jobs almost always demands the background of a college education. Many employers prefer that you have a broad liberal arts background or majors in English, literature, history, philosophy, or one of the social sciences. Other employers desire communications or journalism training in college. Occasionally, a master's degree in a specialized writing field may be required. A number of schools offer courses in journalism, and some of them offer courses or majors in book publishing, publication management, and newspaper and magazine writing.

In addition to formal coursework, most employers look for practical writing experience. If you have served on high school or college newspapers, yearbooks, or literary magazines, you will make a better candidate, as well as if you have worked for small community newspapers or radio stations, even in an unpaid position. Many book publishers, magazines, newspapers, and radio and television stations have summer internship programs that provide valuable training if you want to learn about the publishing and broadcasting businesses. Interns do many simple tasks, such as running errands and answering phones, but some may be asked to perform research, conduct interviews, or even write some minor pieces.

Writers who specialize in technical fields may need degrees, concentrated course work, or experience in specific subject areas. This applies frequently to engineering, business, or one of the sciences. Also, technical communications is a degree now offered at many universities and colleges.

If you wish to enter positions with the federal government, you will have to take a civil service examination and meet certain specified requirements, according to the type and level of position.

Other Requirements

To be a writer, you should be creative and able to express ideas clearly, have a broad general knowledge, be skilled in research techniques, and be computer literate. Other assets include curiosity, persistence, initiative, resourcefulness, and an accurate memory. For some jobs—on a newspaper, for example, where the activity is hectic and deadlines are short—the ability to concentrate and produce under pressure is essential.

EXPLORING

As a high school or college student, you can test your interest and aptitude in the field of writing by serving as a reporter or writer on school newspapers, yearbooks, and literary magazines. Various writing courses and workshops will offer you the opportunity to sharpen your writing skills.

Small community newspapers and local radio stations often welcome contributions from outside sources, although they may not have the resources to pay for them. Jobs in bookstores, magazine shops, and newsstands provide a chance to become familiar with various publications.

You can also obtain information on writing as a career by visiting local newspapers, publishers, or radio and television stations and interviewing some of the writers who work there. Career conferences and other guidance programs frequently include speakers on the entire field of communications from local or national organizations.

EMPLOYERS

There are approximately 126,000 writers and authors, and 57,000 technical writers, currently employed in the United

States. Nearly a fourth of salaried writers and editors work for newspapers, magazines, and book publishers, according to the *Occupational Outlook Handbook*. Writers are also employed by advertising agencies and public relations firms, in radio and television broadcasting, and for journals and newsletters published by business and nonprofit organizations, such as professional associations, labor unions, and religious organizations. Other employers are government agencies and film production companies.

STARTING OUT

A fair amount of experience is required to gain a high-level position in the field. Most writers start out in entry-level positions. These jobs may be listed with college placement offices, or they may be obtained by applying directly to the employment departments of the individual publishers or broadcasting companies. Graduates who previously served internships with these companies often have the advantage of knowing someone who can give them a personal recommendation. Want ads in newspapers and trade journals are another source for jobs. Because of the competition for positions, however, few vacancies are listed with public or private employment agencies.

Employers in the communications field usually are interested in samples of published writing. These are often assembled in an organized portfolio or scrapbook. Bylined or signed articles are more credible (and, as a result, more useful) than stories whose source is not identified.

Beginning positions as a junior writer usually involve library research, preparation of rough drafts for part or all of a report, cataloging, and other related writing tasks. These are generally carried on under the supervision of a senior writer.

Some technical writers have entered the field after working in public relations departments or as technicians or research assistants, then transferring to technical writing as openings occur. Many firms now hire writers directly upon application or recommendation of college professors and placement offices.

Establishing yourself as a full-time novelist is very difficult. Most successful authors start by writing in their free time while relying on a full-time position to pay for their living expenses. Although a full-time position in a writing-related position enables you to hone your writing skills, some authors find that working in a nonwriting field keeps their creative energy in reserve. This helps them focus on writing and submitting works for publication in their free time.

ADVANCEMENT

Most writers find their first jobs as editorial or production assistants. Advancement may be more rapid in small companies, where beginners learn by doing a bit of everything and may be given writing tasks immediately. In large firms, duties are usually more compartmentalized. Assistants in entry-level positions are assigned such tasks as research, fact checking, and copywriting, but it generally takes much longer to advance to full-scale writing duties.

Promotion into more responsible positions may come with the assignment of more important articles and stories to write, or it may be the result of moving to another company. Mobility among employees in this field is common. An assistant in one publishing house may switch to an executive position in another. Or a writer may switch to a related field as a type of advancement.

A technical writer can be promoted to positions of responsibility by moving from such jobs as writer to technical editor to project leader or documentation manager. Opportunities in specialized positions also are possible.

Freelance or self-employed writers earn advancement in the form of larger fees as they gain exposure and establish their reputations.

EARNINGS

In 2002, median annual earnings for salaried writers and authors were $42,790 a year, according to the Bureau of Labor Statistics. The lowest 10 percent earned less than

$21,320, while the highest 10 percent earned $85,140 or more. In book publishing, some specialties pay better than others. Technical writers earned a median salary of $50,580 in 2002.

In addition to their salaries, many writers earn income from freelance work. Part-time freelancers may earn from $5,000 to $15,000 a year. Freelance earnings vary widely. Full-time established freelance writers may earn up to $75,000 a year.

WORK ENVIRONMENT

Working conditions vary for writers. Although their workweek usually runs 35–40 hours, many writers work overtime. A publication issued frequently has more deadlines closer together, creating greater pressures to meet them. The work is especially hectic on newspapers and at broadcasting companies, which operate seven days a week. Writers often work nights and weekends to meet deadlines or to cover a late-developing story.

Most writers work independently, but they often must cooperate with artists, photographers, rewriters, and advertising people who may have widely differing ideas of how the materials should be prepared and presented.

Physical surroundings range from comfortable private offices to noisy, crowded newsrooms filled with other workers typing and talking on the telephone. Some writers must confine their research to the library or telephone interviews, but others may travel to other cities or countries or to local sites, such as theaters, ballparks, airports, factories, or other offices.

The work is arduous, but most writers are seldom bored. Some jobs, such as that of the foreign correspondent, require travel. The most difficult element is the continual pressure of deadlines. People who are the most content as writers enjoy and work well with deadline pressure.

OUTLOOK

The employment of writers is expected to grow at an average rate over the next several years, according to the U.S. Department of Labor. The demand for writers by newspapers, periodicals, book publishers, and nonprofit organizations is expected to increase. The growth of online publishing on company websites and other online services will also demand many talented writers; those with computer skills will be at an advantage as a result. Advertising and public relations will also provide job opportunities.

The major book and magazine publishers, broadcasting companies, advertising agencies, public relations firms, and the federal government account for the concentration of writers in large cities such as New York, Chicago, Los Angeles, Boston, Philadelphia, San Francisco, and Washington, D.C. Opportunities with small newspapers, corporations, and professional, religious, business, technical, and trade publications can be found throughout the country.

People entering this field should realize that the competition for jobs is extremely keen. Beginners may especially have difficulty finding employment. Of the thousands who graduate each year with degrees in English, journalism, communications, and the liberal arts and intend to establish a career as a writer, many turn to other occupations when they find that applicants far outnumber the job openings available. College students would do well to keep this in mind and prepare for an unrelated alternate career in the event they are unable to obtain a position as writer; another benefit of this approach is that, at the same time, they will become qualified as writers in a specialized field. The practicality of preparing for alternate careers is borne out by the fact that opportunities are best in firms that prepare business and trade publications and in technical writing.

Potential writers who end up working in a different field may be able to earn some income as freelancers, selling articles, stories, books, and possibly TV and movie scripts, but it is usually difficult for anyone to be self-supporting entirely on independent writing.

TO LEARN MORE ABOUT WRITERS AND WRITING

BOOKS

Arana, Marie, Ed. *The Writing Life: Writers on How They Think and Work. A Collection from the Washington Post Book World.* New York: PublicAffairs, 2003.

Cowden, Tami D., Caro LaFever, and Sue Viders. *The Complete Writer's Guide to Heroes and Heroines.* Los Angeles: Lone Eagle Publishing Company, 2000.

Gardner, John. *The Art of Fiction: Notes on Craft for Young Writers.* New York: Vintage, 1991.

Goldberg, Natalie. *Writing Down the Bones: Freeing the Writer Within.* Boston, Mass.: Shambhala, 1986.

Van Belkom, Edo. *Writing Horror.* Bellingham, Wash.: Self Counsel Press, 2000.

Zinsser, William K. *On Writing Well: The Classic Guide to Writing Nonfiction.* New York: HarperResource, 2001.

ORGANIZATIONS AND WEBSITES

For information on writing and editing careers in the field of communications, contact

National Association of Science Writers

PO Box 890

Hedgesville, WV 25427

Tel: 304-754-5077

http://www.nasw.org

This organization offers student memberships for those interested in opinion writing.

National Conference of Editorial Writers

3899 North Front Street

Harrisburg, PA 17110

Tel: 717-703-3015

Email: ncew@pa-news.org

http://www.ncew.org

The following website is a great source of information on the writing industry, including helpful advice from editors, agents, and writers of all kinds. Here you can also order the most recent edition of *Writer's Market,* an annual publication that lists contact information for thousands of publishing companies, agents, and magazines.

http://www.writersmarket.com

TO LEARN MORE ABOUT J.K. ROWLING

BOOKS

Campbell, Janis and Cathy Collison. *Authors by Request: An Inside Look at Your Favorite Writers*. Hillsboro, Oregon: Beyond Words, 2002.

Compson, William. *J.K. Rowling*. New York: The Rosen Publishing Group, 2003.

Fraser, Lindsey. *Conversations with J.K. Rowling*. New York: Scholastic, 2001.

Kirk, Connie Ann. *J.K. Rowling: A Biography*. Westport, Connecticut: Greenwood Press, 2003.

McCarthy, Shaun. *All about J.K. Rowling*. Chicago: Raintree, 2004.

Shapiro, Marc. *J.K. Rowling: The Wizard Behind Harry Potter*. New York: St. Martin's Griffin, 2000.

Shields, Charles J. *Mythmaker: The Story of J.K. Rowling*. Broomall, Pennsylvania: Chelsea House Publishers, 2002.

Steffens, Bradley. *J.K. Rowling*. San Diego: Lucent Books, 2002.

WEBSITES

Harry Potter: Meet J.K. Rowling

http://www.scholastic.com/harrypotter/author/
The official website of Rowling's U.S. publisher features a lot of information about her and her books.

JK Rowling

http://www.kidsreads.com/harrypotter/jkrowling.html
Features a transcript of an online interview with Rowling.

Profile: JK Rowling

http://www.januarymagazine.com/profiles/jkrowling.html
An in-depth article about Rowling and her work.

VIDEO

The Magical World of Harry Potter: The Unauthorized Story of J.K. Rowling. Eaton Entertainment, 2000.

This video biography of Rowling's life includes some of her public appearances, interviews with people who know her, and comments from schoolchildren about the *Harry Potter* books.

INDEX

Page numbers in *italics* indicate illustrations.

ABOUT THE AUTHOR

Joanne Mattern is the author of more than 125 books for children. She likes writing nonfiction because it lets her bring real people and events to life. She enjoys music, reading, baseball, animals, travel, and speaking to school and community groups about the topics in her books. She lives in New York State with her husband, two young daughters, and three crazy cats.